Lucy's
Little Book of Advice

CI

RA

First published in 2001 by
Ravette Publishing Limited, Unit 3, Tristar Centre,
Star Road, Partridge Green, West Sussex RH13 8RA

Edited by Gordon Volke

Printed in Malta by Gutenberg Press

ISBN: 1 84161 101 8

Lucy is in love with only two people – the foremost being Lucy.

She cherishes her crabbiness which has been polished into an art-form. She is bossy and loud and grouchy and beautiful.

Lucy is perfect – at least in Lucy's eyes!

Lucy's wisdom gives her the right to charge Charlie Brown for advice, to criticise everything the Literary Ace writes, to torment Linus about his security blanket and thumb-sucking and to teach her baby brother – Rerun, everything.

What Lucy will never be able to accept though, is the fact that her love for Schroeder will never be returned – no matter how 'enchantingly' she drapes herself over the top of his toy piano.

Don't blame people
who are born with
crabby genes.

What are friends for if you can't forget them?

If no one answers the phone,
dial louder.

And when all else fails,
blame it on the media.

If life seems to have
more questions than answers,
try to be the one
who asks the questions.

Birthday presents from Grandma are a problem. The sweaters are too big and the money is too small.

Sidewalks always win ...
knees always lose!

I'm entitled to my opinion and you're entitled to my opinion!

There's a very fine line
between love and hate!

I never think about the past and I never worry about the future, but the present drives me crazy!

Mention marriage to a musician
and you get drowned out!

Isn't this a face
you can trust?

Why shouldn't I complain?
It's the only thing I'm
really good at.

To everything there is a season ... and a time to pull away the football.

No matter how hard you try,
you can't build a rainman.

I suppose I could be nicer to people if I really tried ... but I'd hate to give the rest of the world that satisfaction!

Fun is good enjoyment.

If you want to write a
love letter that shows you
really like a girl, say,
"Enclosed please find a cookie"!

Yelling at your brother three times is one more than the recommended daily allowance.

I'll treat any patient who has a problem and a nickel!

... but is it art?

I've read nine books in a row without understanding any of them.

All the best coaches
are in the stands.

I enjoy being
the bearer of bad news!

Of all the people
I've ever met,
I like me the best!

Women are superior to men, so I get five more. Also, I'm cuter, so that's worth another five. Doesn't that seem fair?

How sharper than
a serpent's tooth
is a sister's "See?"

What's the sense in doing something if you can't get a new record?

Never in all my life did I expect to play second fiddle to a metronome!

Get out of my way –
I got up on the wrong side
of my vitamin pill!

Being crabby all day
makes you hungry.

Peace of mind
would drive me crazy.

I come from a very important family – it's got me in it!

My grandfather always said
that if you read too many
books, your head
would fall off.

If you don't got it,
you don't have it.

I'm too feminine
for football!

If you hold your hands upside-down, you get the opposite of what you pray for.

I've made a lot of mistakes in my days, but I'm going to do something about it ... I'll try to think of some excuses.

It's always difficult to talk
from one generation
to another.

The more I study, the more I realise how little I know – maybe I just shouldn't show up tomorrow.

If they go on a cruise and don't get kissed, it's always the travel agent's fault.

The pen may be mightier
than the sword,
but not a sister's mouth.

I'm not good at names,
but I never forget a slight.

You can't sulk in
a dining room chair.

A hug is better than
all the theology in
the world.

Other books available in this series ...
@ £2.50 each

Charlie Brown's Little Book of Wisdom
ISBN: 1 84161 099 2

Snoopy's Little Book of Laughter
ISBN: 1 84161 100 X

Peppermint Patty's Little Book of Blunders
ISBN: 1 84161 102 6

ЯR
RAVETTE PUBLISHING
Unit 3, Tristar Centre, Star Road, Partridge Green,
West Sussex RH13 8RA